# Birds

ANIMAL FACTS

by Heather C. Hudak

WEIGL PUBLISHERS INC.

Published by Weigl Publishers Inc.
350 5th Avenue, Suite 3304, PMB 6G
New York, NY 10118-0069 USA
Web site: www.weigl.com

Copyright 2005 WEIGL PUBLISHERS INC.
All rights reserved. No part of this publication may be reproduced, stored
in a retrieval system, or transmitted in any form or by any means, electronic,
mechanical, photocopying, recording, or otherwise, without the prior written
permission of the publisher.

Library of Congress Cataloging-in-Publication Data

Hudak, Heather C., 1975-
  Birds / Heather C. Hudak.
      p. cm. -- (Animal facts)
  Includes index.
  ISBN 1-59036-203-9 (library binding : alk. paper) 1-59036-242-X (softcover)
  1. Birds--Juvenile literature. I. Title.
  QL676.H85 2004
  598--dc22
                                  2004002976

                    Printed in the United States of America
                    1 2 3 4 5 6 7 8 9 0   08 07 06 05 04

**Project Coordinator** Heather C. Hudak  **Substantive Editor** Janice L. Redlin
**Copy Editor** Tina Schwartzenberger  **Design** Janine Vangool
**Layout** Bryan Pezzi  **Photo Researcher** Ellen Bryan

**Photograph and Text Credits**
Every reasonable effort has been made to trace ownership and to obtain
permission to reprint copyright material. The publishers would be pleased
to have any errors or omissions brought to their attention so that they may
be corrected in subsequent printings.

**Cover:** Photos.com; **Corel Corporation:** pages 9, 11L, 12, 16, 20, 22, 23; **Eileen Herrling:** page 3; **Dan Nedrelo:** page 15B; **DigitalVision:** page 18; **Photos.com:** pages 1, 5, 6, 7T, 10, 11R, 13, 14T, 14B, 17L, 17T, 19R, 21; **A.B. Sheldon:** page 17B; **Tom Stack & Associates/Dave Watts:** page 4; **J.D. Taylor:** pages 7B, 8, 15T; **U.S. Fish & Wildlife Service:** page 19L (S. Frier).

All of the Internet URLs given in the book were valid at the time of publication.
However, due to the dynamic nature of the Internet, some addresses may have
changed, or sites may have ceased to exist since publication. While the author
and publisher regret any inconvenience this may cause readers, no responsibility
for any such changes can be accepted by either the author or the publisher.

# Contents

What Is a Bird? . . . . . . . . . . . . . . . . . . . 4

Bird Breeds . . . . . . . . . . . . . . . . . . . . 6

Beautiful Birds . . . . . . . . . . . . . . . . . 8

Bird Backgrounds . . . . . . . . . . . . . . 10

Life Cycle . . . . . . . . . . . . . . . . . . . . . 12

Bird Houses . . . . . . . . . . . . . . . . . . . 14

Bird Bites . . . . . . . . . . . . . . . . . . . . . 16

Threatened Birds . . . . . . . . . . . . . . 18

Activities . . . . . . . . . . . . . . . . . . . . . 20

Quiz . . . . . . . . . . . . . . . . . . . . . . . . . 22

Further Reading/Web Sites . . . . . . . . 23

Glossary/Index . . . . . . . . . . . . . . . . 24

# What Is a Bird?

Male emus sit on eggs until they hatch. Male emus care for their young for as long as 2 years.

**B**irds are animals with feathers. All birds have feathers. They are the only animals that have feathers. Birds have wings, too. Most birds can fly. Others run very fast or swim. The emu does not fly. Instead, it can run at speeds up to 30 miles (48.2 kilometers) per hour. The emu can also swim.

Birds live all over the world. They live in many **habitats**. Some birds live in cold places such as mountain. Others live on water banks. Many of these birds **migrate** each year. They return when the weather becomes warmer.

Birds have lived on Earth for millions of years. Today, there are more than 9,000 bird **species**. Each bird species has special features. These features help them to survive in different climates and habitats.

**Bald eagles live only in North America. More than half of the world's bald eagles live in Alaska.**

## Fast Facts

Ornithology is the study of birds.

Hummingbirds can fly backward and sideways.

The bald eagle is the national symbol of the United States.

Ostrich eggs weigh about 3 pounds (1.4 kg). They are the largest bird eggs.

# Bird Breeds

There are two major groups of birds. One group is called *neognathae*. This means they are advanced fliers. The other group is called *palaeognathae*. This means they are flightless birds. Birds are not the only flying animals. Bats and insects fly, too.

**Flocks of Canada geese often fly in a "v" shape. Some geese migrate south for the winter, while other geese stay in the same place year round.**

Most modern birds are **advanced fliers**. These birds have a **keeled** breastbone. Wing muscles attach to the keel. Birds use these muscles to fly. Advanced fliers are lightweight animals. They have long wings, which have a special shape. Wings allow them to fly. Advanced fliers use their wings to fly away from **predators**. They fly when they hunt and migrate, too.

**Flightless birds** have a flat keel. These birds have shorter wings, too. Flightless birds often live on islands where there are few predators. These birds travel by other means. Some swim. Others run. Some can run and swim. Ostriches cannot fly. They can run faster than any other bird. Ostriches can run up to 43 miles per hour (70 kilometers per hour). Ostriches, such as the one pictured left, have claws on their feet to protect against predators.

# Beautiful Birds

Birds come in many shapes and sizes. Still, all birds share some body features. All birds have feathers. These feathers are called plumage. Some birds have plumage that blends into their environment. This helps them hide from predators. Ptarmigans change color with the seasons. Their feathers turn white in the winter to match the snow. Their plumage is brown in the summer to match plants and trees.

Peacocks are male peafowl. They are one of the most colorful bird species. They are part of the pheasant and turkey family.

All birds have a bill, two legs, and wings. Birds use their bills to **preen**. Preening removes oil and **parasites** from a bird's feathers. Birds have four toes. These toes help birds perch, climb, swim, and hunt. Wings can be long or short, pointed or round. The way a bird flies depends on its wing shape. Some birds soar. Others glide or flap.

Most birds have a tail. They use their tail to control their direction when flying. It also helps control landings. Male peacocks use their tail feathers to attract mates. The male peacock has a colorful spread of feathers he displays for female peacocks.

Many birds have a syrinx. This is a voice box, which allows birds to make sounds. Some birds also sing. Wood thrushes can sing two songs at the same time.

In the early 1900s, few wood ducks remained. Today, there are more than one million wood ducks in North America.

## Fast Facts

Some birds are very small. Bee hummingbirds are the smallest birds. They are 2.5 inches (6.4 centimeters) long and weigh 0.06 ounces (1.7 grams). Other birds are very large. The ostrich is the largest bird. It stands 9 feet (2.7 meters) tall.

Most adult birds molt at least once each year. This means they lose and replace their feathers.

Birds have well-developed brains.

Birds have lightweight skeletons. Many of their bones are hollow. This helps them fly.

# Bird Backgrounds

Scientists use **fossils** to learn about animal history. Scientists believe flying animals lived about 200 million years ago. These flying dinosaurs were called *pterosaurs*. They had wings, but they did not have feathers. Many of these animals died with the dinosaurs. The *Pterodactyl* is a well-known pterosaur. Some Pterodactyls were about the size of a pigeon. Others had a wing span longer than 40 feet (12.2 meters). They used their long noses to dig for worms.

**Scientists believe that when Pterodactyls were not flying they walked on all four legs.**

Scientists believe the first birds developed from pterosaurs. The first birds appeared about 150 million years ago. They were called *Archaeopteryx*. Like modern birds, the Archaeopteryx had feathers. It had light, hollow bones, too. Like reptiles, the Archaeopteryx had teeth and claws on its wings.

**Scientists are not certain about Archaeopteryx's appearance. They use fossils and research to learn more about this animal.**

**Many scientists believe that the Archaeopteryx did not fly well. Some believe it glided down from trees. Others believe it ran after its prey.**

## Fast Facts

The first Archaeopteryx fossil was found in 1860. Archaeopteryx is Latin for ancient wing.

The first modern birds appeared about 65 million years ago. They were the ancestors of ducks and flamingos.

# Life Cycle

Most birds care for their young. Parents bring food to their babies and teach them how to fly.

**B**irds hatch from eggs. Female birds produce eggs. The male bird **fertilizes** the eggs inside the female's body. The female lays the eggs in a **clutch** after mating. Some birds lay only one egg. Others lay up to 20 eggs.

Most birds sit on their eggs. This keeps the eggs warm. This is called incubation. Incubation may last between 10 days and 2.5 months. Baby birds are called chicks. Many chicks are featherless and blind at birth. These birds include pelicans and woodpeckers. Some chicks are born with feathers and can see. They can swim or run, too. These birds include geese, swans, and turkeys.

Chicks become fledglings after they develop **flight feathers**. Fledglings explore, but they still rely on their parents for food. Most fledglings can survive on their own after they have been out of the nest for about 2 weeks.

Often, birds are fully grown within a few months to 1 year. The peregrine falcon is fully grown by 6 weeks of age. Other birds are fully grown by 2 to 3 years of age. Some take longer to mature. The male magnificent bird of paradise is full grown between 3 and 6 years old.

**Sea gulls build nests on cliffs and islands to protect their young from weather and predators.**

# Bird Houses

Birds live in every part of the world. Some live near water. These birds can float on the water or swim. Birds that hunt other animals live in open fields and prairies. Many small birds live near trees, bushes, and tall grass. These birds can hide and nest in these areas. Others, such as the snowy owl and the tufted puffin, live in the cold **arctic tundra**.

Tropical tanagers are brightly colored birds that live in the American tropics. These birds live in trees and shrubby areas.

Painted storks live in freshwater marshes and ponds in India, Vietnam, Sri Lanka, Cambodia, Thailand, and eastern China. These birds wade in shallow water. They swing their heads under the water to find fish and frogs to eat.

**The golden tanager lives in South America.**

**Tufted puffins breed on islands in the northern Pacific ocean.**

Turkey vultures live throughout North America. These birds are found in dry, open fields and ranchlands. Turkey vultures eat dead animals, or carrion. Some live near roads where carrion is often found.

**When threatened, turkey vultures vomit. This makes the bird weigh less. It may also frighten predators.**

**Saddle-billed storks are the largest African stork. They often live near water.**

## Fast Facts

Birds feet and bills are adapted to the places where they live. Swimming birds, such as loons, have webbed feet to help them move through water. Perching birds, such as sparrows, have a long hind toe. This toe helps these birds grip their perch. Some birds, such as woodpeckers, have long, pointed bills called chisel bills. They use their bills to drill into trees.

# Bird Bites

Most birds are carnivores. This means they are meat-eating animals. Many birds eat insects. Others eat fish or meat. Some birds eat both meat and seeds. Blue jays eat seeds and berries such as blueberries. They eat rodents, lizards, insects, and other birds, too.

**Blue jays can store food, such as seeds and nuts, in their throats.**

Insect-eating birds catch their meals in the air. Birds search for insects on tree bark, leaves, twigs, and stems, too. Whippoorwills are nocturnal. This means they are active at night. They eat only insects such as grasshoppers, beetles, and night-flying moths.

Some bird species eat seeds or fruit. Grass, elm, and sunflowers are just some of the seeds birds eat. Pigeons eat mostly fruit and seeds. Many seed-eating birds eat some insects, too. The common grackle eats insects as well as fruit and seeds.

**Owls are birds of prey. This means they eat living animals, such as mice, moles, fish, and rabbits.**

**Bee-eaters eat bees, wasps, and hornets. They hit the insect against a hard surface to remove the sting.**

## Fast Facts

Birds do not have teeth. This means they cannot chew their food. They cut food with their bills or swallow it whole.

Birds must eat large amounts of food so they have enough energy to fly. Some small birds eat more than their own weight in food everyday.

**Sometimes, common grackles eat small birds and lizards. They also eat bird's eggs.**

# Threatened Birds

**A**nimals that are in danger of becoming **extinct** are called endangered. This means that there are so few of the species that they need protection in order to survive. People are not allowed to hunt endangered species in the United States.

There are more than 200 species of endangered birds in the world. In some cases, their habitat has become too **polluted** and unhealthy. Other habitats have disappeared. Some birds have been overhunted for their feathers. **Pesticides** have poisoned some food supplies. The poison can cause eggshells to become so thin they crack during incubation.

Oil can stick to a bird's feathers, making it impossible for it to fly. Birds can also become poisoned if they eat oil as they clean themselves.

There are about 65 species of endangered birds in the United States. Most of these birds live in Hawai'i. Birds such as the Hawai'ian honeycreeper and the nene face loss of habitat. Humans are building in the areas where these birds live. The California condor and the whooping crane are other birds that have been harmed by human development in the United States.

The Hawai'ian moorhen is one of 29 threatened and endangered birds living on the Hawai'ian islands.

**In the 1970s, there were about 30 California condors.**

## Fast Facts

The Hawaii Endangered Bird Conservation Program began in 1993. The program helps increase the number of babies born to twelve species of endangered Hawai'ian birds.

The imperial woodpecker is the largest species of woodpecker. It lives in the tropical rain forests of Mexico. It was last seen in 1993.

# Activities

## Feathered Friends

Birds are the only animals that have feathers. Birds use feathers to fly and blend into their environments. Feathers keep birds warm, too. Small, fluffy feathers called down keep birds warm. The following activity shows how feathers keep birds warm.

**Materials**

- funnel
- water
- two balloons
- two plastic bags
- freezer
- down feathers
- dull knife
- measuring cup
- pen

1. Use a funnel to fill two balloons with the same amount of water. Make sure the balloons do not stretch too much.

2. Place both balloons in the freezer. Remove the balloons from the freezer once they are frozen.

3. Place one balloon in an empty plastic bag. Place the other balloon in a down-filled plastic bag.

4. Let the bags sit for 60 to 90 minutes. What do you think will happen to the balloons?

5. Use the dull knife to cut open each balloon. Pour the melted water in the measuring cup. Which balloon held more melted water? What did the feathers do to the ice?

The belted kingfisher has a crest of feathers on its head. These feathers keep the bird warm as it fishes for food.

20

# Ruffled Feathers

Sometimes boats spill oil in water. Oil spills harm birds. Oil settles on birds' feathers. This means they cannot keep afloat. Often birds drown. The following activity shows what happens to birds during an oil spill.

### Materials

- two pans
- water
- feathers
- cooking oil
- mild dish soap
- paper towels

1. Fill both pans with 4 to 5 inches (10.16 to 12.7 centimeters) of water.

2. Place a feather in one of the water pans. What happens?

3. Pour cooking oil in the other water pan. What happens to the water?

4. Place a feather in the oil and water mixture. What happens to the feather?

5. Place the feather from the oil and water mixture in the water pan. What happens to the feather now?

6. Try cleaning the feather with water. Does the feather float?

7. Try cleaning the feather with mild dish soap. Does the feather float?

# Quiz

**What have you learned about birds? See if you can answer the following questions correctly.**

1. What is the difference between advanced fliers and flightless birds?

2. What are baby birds called?

3. How long have birds lived on Earth?

4. Name two threats to birds.

5. What two special body features do all birds have?

**Egrets use their long legs and powerful necks to quickly snatch fish from shallow water.**

**Answers:** 1. Advanced fliers have a keeled breastbone. Flightless birds have a flat keel. 2. Baby birds are called chicks. 3. Birds have lived on Earth for 150 million years. 4. Pesticides and human development threaten birds. 5. All birds have wings, feathers, a bill, and two legs.

# Further Reading

Boring, Mel, and Linda Garrow (illustrator). *Birds, Nests and Eggs*. Chanhassen, MN: NorthWord Press, 1998.

Herkert, Barbara (illustrator). *Birds in Your Backyard*. Bt Bound, 2002.

Kittinger, Jo S. *Smithsonian Kids' Field Guides: Birds of North America East*. New York, NY: DK Publishing, 2001.

# Web Sites

For more information about birds, surf www.enchantedlearning.com/subjects/birds

To learn about birds of the world, visit www.birds.cornell.edu

**The yellow-shafted flicker is a type of woodpecker. Flickers can hollow out parts of trees with their strong bills. They build their nests in dead tree trunks or branches.**

# Glossary

**arctic tundra** a very cold, treeless area in the far northern areas of North America and Asia

**clutch** a set of eggs produced at the same time

**extinct** no longer living

**fertilizes** makes another animal able to produce young

**flight feathers** tail, wing, and body feathers

**fossils** rocklike remains of ancient plants and animals

**habitats** places where animals live in nature

**keeled** having a lengthwise structure on a bone

**migrate** to move from one place to another

**parasites** living things that grow, feed, and live on another living thing

**pesticides** chemicals used to kill pests

**polluted** made dirty and unhealthy with waste

**predators** animals that hunt other animals for food

**preen** to smooth or clean with the bill

**species** type or sort

# Index

**advanced fliers** 6, 7, 22

**bills** 9, 15, 17, 22, 23

**California condor** 19

**emu** 4, 5
**endangered** 18, 19

**feathers** 5, 8, 9, 10, 11, 13, 18, 20, 21, 22
**feet** 7, 15
**flightless birds** 6, 7, 22

**habitats** 5, 18, 19

**life cycle** 12, 13

**migrate** 5, 6, 7

**oil** 9, 18, 21
**ostrich** 7, 9

**tanagers** 14

**wings** 5, 7, 9, 10, 11, 22